In | Between

Angela Arnold

Stairwell Books //

Published by Stairwell Books
161 Lowther Street
York, YO31 7LZ

www.stairwellbooks.co.uk
@stairwellbooks

In | Between © 2023 Angela Arnold and Stairwell Books

All rights reserved. No part of this publication may be reproduced, stored in or introduced into a retrieval system, or transmitted, in any form, or by any means (electronic, mechanical, photocopying, recording, e-book or otherwise) without the prior written permission of the author.

The moral rights of the author have been asserted.

Cover Image: *Narrow passage of rocks of Petra Canyon in Wadi Musa, Jordan*: astudio

ISBN: 978-1-913432-72-0

Acknowledgements

Glass Darkly first published in The Interpreter's House, issue 63
Some Other Time first published in Popshot, issue 25
The Knowledge of Silver first published in Marble, issue 5
One Hell of an Amateur Uncle first published in the anthology *Mill* by Templar Poetry (2015)
Glimpse and *She has to Do Things Brightly* first published in OWP, issue 91
A Burning to be published by Black Sunflowers in their anthology *Fire* (2023)

Table of Contents

In

They	2
She Has to Do Things Brightly	3
Clothing the Soul	4
The Bad Words	5
Something to Give	6
Glimpse	7
All the Love on the Train	8
In Cardland	9
Heads and Hands	10
Jogging off the Past, to Be Honest	11
How to Be Shut	12
What Do I Call You?	13
Grave to Shear	14
Some Other Time	15
Here	16
Write It Down	17
He, Still	19
When	20
The Knowledge of Silver	21
Years of Her	22
News	23
Driving Round Decisionshire	24
Standing Still on Empty	25
Called	26
Not Moving	27
Glass Darkly	28
The Braver Violence of Dreams	29
Other Feet	31
Colours to Go	32
True Eucalyptus	33

Being Lovely	34
For the First Time	35
Milk, of All Things	36
The 13 O'Clock News	37
The Word Child	38
Acting It	39
Alive	40
Staying In	41

Between

Thief	43
Seen	44
Face to Face	45
One Hell of an Amateur Uncle	46
Picking a Replacement	47
Closer	48
Different Planet	49
Masks Before Masks	50
Screwdriver	52
A Burning	53
Book	54
Not Saying	55
Looking For	56
Spine Chillers	57
Strangers in Time	58
The Light in your Eyes	59
Lying Somewhere Else	60
Twelve Plates Spinning	61
Gathering the Us	62
New Co-Ordinates	63
Winding Up	64
Gone. And Gone.	65
At a Gate	66
The DNA Says	67
Ghost	68

The Safety of No-One	69
Never Saw Me	70
Voiceless	71
The Sand Underfoot	72
Don't Shoot the Owl	73
The Real Rat	74
Earth People	75
Other Others	76
A Whole Load of Space	77
Rules	79
Counting	80
Blue Fingers	81
Today, in the Plaza	82

In

They

Spider, spider on the wall
shinning up, knocking on deaf
window after window with your long
scimitar legs, glossy slate and sharp and too quick.
And far too many – a multitude by yourself.

You weave your out-
of-this-world nests, eggs, nodules
that will contain, again, unknown multitudes; weave
the very protestations of the man who dunnit
before you spiderly tippy-toe off,
leaving threats today, tomorrow lies
on ripped-out pages
or a sarcasm of unattended dishes.

It is impossible
now to open windows, lest cries
fly in to build nests of their own, stuff them
with half-breeds (part malice,
part helplessness) and impurities
of recollection.
Self-serving, self-preserving figments: webs
that properly snarl, if they put their mind to it.
Webs that keep; busy, busy.

Spider, spider outside my mirror
window, look deeply.
I have a long stick handy
for when winter comes, when
cold enough is what the diary could safely say.

She Has to Do Things Brightly

With every inch of her heart. Let her be.
To dance down the street with red-twinkling feet
and a cloak to match that will never just
button, that would be merely literal –
hers is a much sharper living
out of the rich well of her.
Other to the power of banged trumpets,
with drum rolls that wash ashore, wash ashore, with
something sublimely missing:
this plain lovable bluntness totally takes
the edge off you and me. Let her be.
Her flighty voice carries
everything that ought to be afoot
in a proper world.
Her gestures expand all the world's volumes
spoken, by a factor of x.
Her giggles say brakes are for those of us
who don't know how to die.
She is all of us, burning.

Clothing the Soul

An open wardrobe – an hour – a question
avoided, always.

Mother, wondering, huffing, stripey thing, she suggests,
but then she has aspirations, notions
of normal.
Only refrain father can offer is like something
dragged in, but that's regardless, no pleasing him.

Pleasing in blue, red, green, in tight-lipped, in baggy and
leggy and flouncily flaunting, showing them
precisely nothing
of self. –
Wear it, tear it off again; paint yourself, slap it on, floor to
ceiling, for others to live in. Question still not
approached, not found its words yet, inside,
in head's own wardrobe.
Don't even say 'binary'.

How difficult can it be? Cloth. Mask. Act. Please.
No doors or windows needed. Live, just
like every other captive. ⁄⁄

The Bad Words

She courts them, the cursers and spitters
of swear words. The filth
that doesn't *quite* ripen into deeds.

Though who knows how many twisted mis-
doings as well: the shame of them illuminating her day,
who knows why. She's a picture of thoughtfulness, otherwise.

Maybe she hopes to sow something,
with her presence;
or take who knows what with her, into her wordless days,

her lone furrow – things that will fertilise the very
ground, foul dirt deep into the common soil – something
will come of it.

Something good even.
For now, the precious seeds of discomfort press, up-heave
like yeast having the last word;

and she gives ten-mile smiles at the Fucks that miss
their target. – The shouters blink her away. Tellingly.
But still she rakes it all in as she goes, taking care.

Something to Give

'Lend me your gentler heart', I said
and you laughed, said 'Grow your own' as if
one could womb one up
from the depths, out of the left-over beginnings.

'It's fundamentally unfair', I said, thinking of all the
loveable ones, the unshunned of the world:
our swiftly forgiving heroines – who give
screaming abuse a miss, gifted as they are

Bred like that. Radiating the willingness to cook and
iron time away with no complaint
and take armfuls of concern to their neighbours, clearly
made like that from the off. The effortlessly

faithful husbands with a smile that is both nine
and ninety rolled into one indisputable
loveableness. – All those.
The unfairness of it, to us: who else

will set light to yesterday's applecarts, get out
the pneumatic drill mid-speech, tip the balance
between bath water and surplus baby.
The smiles we raise may be belated. Give us time. ⁄⁄

Glimpse

Old man naked, unaware
of the door cracked open, the window
still as bare as himself and
star gazing neighbour left in shock – touched
by something unexpected. Seeing
only a self revealed that's here-now quite
inexplicably other.

One who visits only in the company
of weirdness, stress, surprise, at thoroughly
wrong-footed times.

A bear self perhaps, unpredictable.
Or a slinking fox
sticking to the hidden gullies and hollows
of experience, the better to gorge.

She stares, this something different scenting animal,
gobbling a feast of embarrassment and slyness
and transgression magnified
by the length and depth
of the stare, the spread
of the blush, in the pitch dark.
The unshared appropriated with such relish.

Promising her twin proper self that this may be
a necessary anthropology of sorts,
this examining of a soul
laid bare in its forgetting.

All the Love on the Train

Du-dums like daisy petals. TugandDrop, TugandDrop.
Like falling answers, discarded as ex. Or else trigger-
finger-poised: all tremble and titter before the plucking.

Petal...courage...question...petal...breath held.
The du-DUMs that make echoes echo echoes: a whole life
of that. And the soft thuds. The endless march

of sliding doors with their exquisite sound of a long regret,
their sigh of a laugh that'll repeatedly dismiss
each One as 1 or 1000 lumbersome milestones ago,

before things derailed – all done now. DuDUMdum.
Gentle enough jolts; soothing
announcements. As if swoosh

through to chug on to heart braking hiss was
normal, and repetition (a fact)
made it quite alright that memory should be substantial

enough to count as love.
Hoots, tunnel: still the same reflection – not one
station ahead peopled either. ⁄⁄

In Cardland

She slits the first envelope like a careful butcher
looking to extract precious innards:
set them aside for later, process, leisurely.

She slits the second more deftly,
hoping for more than hasty ink. But 27 years
have bleached the connection;

computer has winked into action, spewed updates
on a life in bl/wh. She plucks at it, disembowelling
a dictionary in the wrong language. Next.

No more than a neighbour's neighbour (doubly ex now) who
will insist, year after year. Pointlessly faithful.
Counting them? pride? desperation?

Do these cheap, small 2D gifts redeem themselves
through the price of a stamp?
Amount to more than a human cobweb?

She puckers her lips into a mound – think
of all the pens numbly twiddled (what to say?). *Don't*
think of the repetition involved – look

beyond the fancy-fonted round robins. You *could* receive
your customised headings with something
like seasonal grace. – And stop fingering the signature,

even (especially) the daughter's:
won't make the thing at all personal.
"No-Love-Rubs-Off" blade beat-beat-beats on her thigh. ⁂

Heads and Hands

Mother, giant with the booming voice...huge feet that tread-tread the grass flat across an endless green, past a looming of finger wagging trees, her towering stick-gun friends.

Mum with her busy hands:
how she makes a grab
for his fist, arm, sleeve, any
handy fledgeling handle.
To keep in check,
prevent the worst, not let
this little spirit slip his mooring.

Along she goes, shop-rattled already, hand again
on auto pilot
swipes, hooks him, reins him in – a tiny past life doll still
hunkered behind her eyes, visibly
conducting: arm yanked, yanked, while he screams,
screams out
the badness of his power-hungry heart. *MY arm, MY hand, MY park, trees, world, me, MINE!* And it's a stand-off.

Her massive head;
its tiny bird-caged doll.
His little screwed-eyes face as yet
(almost) without hinterland:
preoccupied only with stamping the flat earth and all its
good slobbery mud into pocket-sized craters and
a *ME!*-shaped mess – the terror of that.

Little mum inside the giant mum must, ab-so-lute-ly
must, lift her...lift her baton. Tap out the cries, the cries
that repeat, and go on to repeat. ⁄⁄

Jogging off the Past, to Be Honest

Run-runrun *and* run...on to a proper knee-hurt redemption
if need be. Then stitch-hobble off to a reparation or three,
a howling knee truly nothing, in fleeting comparison.
Put some welly into blistering
chafe up a storm, conjure
real shin splints out of belated regret.
(Though your sins may not be severe enough
to deserve these.)
Blister at a time,
ankle throb after throb,
you can feel your
past thinning – keep running –
just think of the thrill
of a tidily wrenched ankle.

Keep hounding
after this healing fantasy of a hip slipped
gracefully from its moorings:
searing you.

Mind-rattlingly clean –
for the length of a gasp of a dishonest moment
that won't own it all: real You, born

this wretched now. Call it that,
while the pain still sings. ⁄⁄

How to Be Shut

Take a good slap of early years; add a sharp jab
of new school; drizzle with a loving smatter
of adolescent confusion; let it rest. Then follow

with a time-and-again-battered kneading, knead well, all
the mulled married memory of it, stretch it –
warmth, red-faced, will add magic, make it rise

to the occasion, yield. Then chop the whole thing, affair
after affair, into sections, layered with work,
moves, the eventual mirror challenge of kids, still rising,

still painfully stretching. Dollop, dis-connect, let it bake
in the heat of its own multiple shame (a good grilling
from a therapist never touches it). Finally.

The perfect crust. Not a chink. ◢

What Do I Call You?

Wine-eyed, I search again, take stabs at a guess.
Which me: the was, the meant to, the would
if I could – used to. And look: the official version.
A pick & mix past that no doubt
can still brew up
fresh pots of consequences.

Howls about godknowswhat float, effortlessly,
into the picture. So *not* the fairest of them all.

I strain, teeth a pale gleam
and there: a proper grown up take on the theme
to whisper into the broken microphone
of this pisspoor party.
No – really look sleuth-closely now, spot a small
stranger in among, if you can:

Lynne, Lynnie, Lin, Lynda-May, they dance a conga,
ignoring the frame, bust each other's myths
while this putative Other hangs back
nameless. Not asked. Another go:
trying and trawling this silvery lake, though
seriously askew and a-sway.

Windows of the soul? Am I the proud owner
of a fall-back position, if all else fails, fail – every one?
One more everlasting than the candle behind me, on the
wrong side of my other shoulder (just to
confuse matters), without that little old scar left,
or is it right, of my midnight stare?

Grave to Shear

Not nothing.
Just nothing but inexplicable ivy.

Straggle-stuff called 'Peter'. Obliquely related to a jangle of
words...tragedy, son (guiltily, the thing I somehow wasn't),
brother. Words too quiet,
too tightly muttered, while they hacked at you, you bother:
tangle-tying green arms, sticking a hundred feet into soil.

Peter-the-leafy-absence
who keeps growing too much. Peter-the-impatient-haircut,
snake of twiggy bits, gathered and dumped, left there,
the he-puzzle. Him. Never
answering the Scrrrp, Scrrrp, the scissoring Scrrrp. Good

tug and you'll be back soon enough, 'brother',
nowhere boy stuck in your gone time –
in hiding: all airy there
(anywhere? everywhere?) and not a bit green.
Secretly dancing it, your endlessly beginningless tale?
Maybe even where I could see, if I looked,
the proper shape of that name:
in the wind-wild trees, the dazzle of gate,
the black-eyed stones in the wall.

Quite uncuttable there, of course, only mocking
the rude shears, ignoring your
far too late name. ∥

Some Other Time

Clock struck three so slowly, gran, maybe
to suck me in – slowly, slowly –
like the long pasta? And listen: clock
goes with a tickety-tock
limp that's tremendously HUGE, gran. Have you noticed?
Gran? All you ever say is Hush, meaning
sit? still? meaning wait
till time gives us words again?
      making me boil
        very quietly, sit heart-in-mouth
        shrunk, my blood a stutter
        and thunder too
Do you know
your clock has lost two of its teeth?

Your time-diddling secrets
never slip out of your mouth – do they, gran?
Still that clock knocks
at my heart and ticks off its riddles
one after the scary other. I know, *your* time
never rages! I know:

it sticks, stops,
scratches its nose
just like you do, gran,
before it hands over a PILE of seconds – how
they stomp giant boots! – then holds on hard to its breath.

It strikes its six
exactly when you're ready. *Does.*

Here

I hear, do hear you insist, repeat and repeat, shout it
again, yes, that you will (this! or possibly that!) –
but weren't we here a week ago
on a different track, different
shots fired in some other direction?
Your small frame looks as if a much bigger person
was crouched inside, birthing
a massive burn, a fever wielding
a blowtorch, yes: ssssshhhhhh!!

And now your face folds and unfolds like pure paper plans
full of the secrets of world domination/amelioration,
whichever the wide-open-door secret
may be, this week.

The constant there is fire
and target
and motion.
They rattle your child's body like lifequake as such.
Fill and empty you like the sweet floods
of action itself, because.
Because here you are, is all.

Write It Down

Failed to send you a card. So I call... And your name? Not
even a Please tell me again. Not even a lame
Who did you say? Total bluntness:
And Your Name? for the sixth time
in a quarter hour, and I
spell it,
so you can write it down. Again.

How many pieces of paper,
tiny, ragged ones –
I do remember your frugal ways with paper –
how many
fragile shards
of used envelopes are you scribbling
this lost name on?

I'm staring at it down the phone: the hard labour;
disconnect; frequent
apologies; random; you forget
what *for*
and only the odd My memory! or a flash of I Know
that name So well! before another sinkhole swallows
the latest bust light bulb moment –
and. Your. Name.
Well,
you *would* put it like that, your style still
itself, your riddled self still
sounding entirely Jean...? Much harder to shake is the
last memory of calling
in person and you not letting
the stranger in.

Better, much better,
to conduct this (is there a word for it?

has there ever been one?) at a safe distance, giving us
both a chance to feint, wriggle, to-hell-
with-it invent another tack, with something almost
like ease: And your name?
Let me spell it for you. Like never before. ⁄⁄

He, Still

He remembers the fur, blond, black
and rough, and her hair, its long
long feel, the smooth curve from neck
to back, and the small hands reaching,
and long noses on his knee.
He can still smell the musty clinging wetness,
and the showeredness-in-lemon,
the newborn skin in all its heady otherness.
Still all there, in sharp clipped rapid detail –
as if there was a hurry
before the

he even sees something
like new possibilities
shapeless ones
so far –
as if skins
had never
really
mattered

When

When the gulls' cries stop
being mentioned, again and again
and again, what then?

When his cracked shoes have stood there
empty for far too long, *what*
then? Will gulls scream

in my head too, repeat the thing,
scupper the last lovehate connection till I see
only sea; unable to count it,

insist on counting it then and then and then?

The Knowledge of Silver

It's not dirt, you babble, emphatic,
hastily swipe something aside
with a gesture: not dirt.
I know.

The wintry coat the kettle grows and
*re*grows, flakes as you tip; rimes and prime
stain grabbers – tea a speciality, and
spoons that will sport half trans-ethnic moons

all round the rim, whitely silver still
inside. I know what it takes: a sharp
fingernail to groove away,
stubbornly; scourers

only leaving that unspoon smell
of pungent newness –
inappropriate.
But you, you don't scrape, scrape,

scrape; you're content
that all is as should be,
intact, underneath and really,
I would think, maybe

as a husband might
still walk heavy footed,
most midnights,
to the perfect drum of your pulse.

Years of Her

Down past her waist and he suggests –
but she wails.

All the most secret occasions, in the smokiest places,
are thickly captured here

and the greying wisps of promises, sparsely embedded,
still waiting to regrow lustrous.

Her mouth can still reach
the kisses no one remembers now, today

or tomorrow. Her hands can wring them
one more time for life

today, and tomorrow
her cries will be even louder: what he so

bullishly-ill-knowingly suggests
cannot be done

this side of the final lid on it.
Till then each single page of a strand

shall remain immortal: her indecipherable
howls, last gloat of sanity, will see to it.

News

Thank you, said suitably quietly; receiver put *down*.

Try hard not to picture the lane, the bricks, the blazing
semaphore initials (giggles, against all our better
judgement) evidence visible still. Guilty

pleasures unfolded there; an authorless, unscripted, mess:
love in parallel, love dead awkward – a pair of uneasy wings.
Drooped black rags of cormorant drying, hardly belonging.

The sea wasn't far. We could have blamed its push-pull.

To think it was no more than a touch of flitter in the air,
in the beginning. Mutual, those barely
questionable hints. A thin, tidy rigmarole.

Maybe, for a month, a more definitely nothing. Before one
single hot solitary (well, no) afternoon
with every sort of blind tugged shut, windows silent

as the eyes of our twined souls –

windows that need shutters more than ever; instead
roar to be flung open, unthinkable timing.
Honesty demanding to pay

its own respects? A twitch, now, of those bat-black wings
(for decades presumed folded, case shut). Irony.
Inexcusable feelings now, here, all over the table, scattered

like the sweet leftovers.

Driving Round Decisionshire

Caught between you and *you;* one
doubtless offering the smoother face, the gentling smile,
'civilised' in large letters – but,

but...*you* might reveal
other roads. The too full lips, the darknight scrub
of scratchy beard, with its

outbrazening, its mocking
of the donnishly clean-shaven with
its purely comforting, glasses-straightening, thought-out
                                                                      delivery

of an almost, in fact, identical sentence.
One a picture of safe knowns,
not grabbed; not like that.

The other a scrumptious ripple in belly's own spacetime
where the looking at choices, choices,
is the silly pain of it.

To lick at the wild, just
once taste life's bright woolfishness; follow
that *knowing* look to total tilt, warp of hours: not let

flat reason stand to reason.

Standing Still on Empty

She entertains great stacks of them. Square
and snappy, oblong, cloud-water plastic. Stout, round
little things in see-through dresses, all extravagantly

lidded in mauve, sharp green, low moon yellow.
With caps that invite decapitation, roll up, hop in,
let there be life in such socially echoing halls.

Smears of cream cheese invited, suggestive. Perhaps.
An assembly of meaty flakes. Charged remnants
of life. Proof of something (no matter

nothing much did, or does). Meantime, she won't
mind her too many containers brazening
empty, towering ready

for especially nothing. This is peace:
space stored, time preserved. Stocked
tight & secure. Here is all the Life-one-might-lead

not quite yet breathing. To hand, though, to be had,
to be, always, if. Ample. Enough to be giving
birth to, when the time comes. ⁄⁄

Called

Him indoors stretching out his morning tea: wordlessly
leafing page by (teeth sucking) page
through his dryness of papers.

Her out by the back door then. Plenty of pages, reams
of history, green flesh-blood-and-bone documented.

Right here: Jo herself, with her still settling real-deal bulbs
she'd so careful-dentist extracted from the jaws
of a spreading armada of impostors two seasons ago.
A tiny, loud tada! before she left. A company
of husky ghosts are these Jos come July,
precise shedders of life,
heavily shaded (as instructed)
by Helen's no-nonsense Geranium Watchamacallit –
the once son, now in New Zealand, he
should know, being a botanist and all. Probably.

She dawdles on, nods in passing
at the great flourish of Sidalcea (how to pronounce it
always a bone of contention) Sven had urged her to split,
robustly, take a bit, a mere month before
dying. Still here, still bulking up nicely, still
arguing the toss, where to put the stress, 'al'? 'eh'?
She fingers the plump dome of it:
surreptitious caress for a whole society
of glossy green scallops, such an envy of foliage.

In plain enough sight, Eilidh's grass no more than a stab
of sheen in its dark corner; positively singing
with plump offspring. Arresting thought, her just there,
about to scatter a delicate insurrection of footprints.
So many to bear her name.

Not Moving

Borrowed van, a friend's. The moving in (into
what?) no better than piece work, a reluctant drip-drip.
Call it resentment, to be sunk
into a flat present of sea:
an arms-wide sky the only bright thing.

The moving on (on to what?) a grudging heel-drag, years
of feeling old clay coat my fingers, pebbles
slip wetly away, heavy little echoes. Years still hearing
the faint clucking of escapees. More
not mud-surfing round dicey, sharpish corners.

Decades later this huge van, properly organised, paid:
a whole neighbourhood of hands
stuffing it to the gills with boxed pain
and wrapped loss, mattress slotted in like a last
compressed look at the sky –

how else to take it, where else
to park the surprise of near-tears, stow the guilt
of a bigamy of pasts? When exactly did those
trees stake their claim? – When exactly will the reddening
rocks of some future stop being dust in my mouth

and manage to best the clay, the sand, the dotty
pebbles, *that* corner, the shrilly swallow-weighted
wires…this slew of roof bodge drips – cement
that my own determined hand
slung there, and patted: for ever.

Glass Darkly

Three times slowly round car park before I
stop, three o'clock and something right about that.

Only other car a black ghost, its shape
stamped clearly where it had waited, left, after

a small, brisk nightfall of snow. Even the snowing
hushed now. And town clock lost for an opinion.

Muffled humming from tyres, lights processing
past. Nothing that would scissor into the night.

And when snow starts up again, it takes the last
scalp of a footprint from the square, gifts it to me.

When you finally phone, checking the odd lateness
of this party, I say I'm in transit now, on this or that

or even *the* way – isn't that where I am? At least
that much must be true. What else could I say?

The Braver Violence of Dreams

They hack into truth.
Plot urgently to mock a history not all that past (or even
that hidden) and now torn strands are everywhere,
generously litter the floor
of the unexamined memory. Here's one
for Richard, one for John, and Phillip, Terry,
Michael – all dead easy
threads to string into constantly updated tales.
Love snipped, love chopped
into short filaments and free
to enter newish narratives. (Lies, if you prefer.)

Night has different uses.
Now it has love lit.
Love rendered.
A trip to the cellars far beneath
the story. Bleached of the colour of the original feeling.
With inexplicable editorial decisions – impossible
to own, in the morning.

The locked-into-a-cupboard-and-left-to-starve take.
The testing an un-responsive body sequel, weeks later,
just a different guise. A splintered tale
of ice floes sent to take what, who, mattered the most
out into a purple-stroked sea.
A twisted escaping-from version, with a staircase that's
endless, and endless and then never ending because
waking throws a spanner.
The mental chill

that is so, apparently, unfair.
What roadless country harbours these real extensions
to the house you actually built? How
is it even all yours? Where
was such picked-bare-bones courage hatched, mined? ⁄⁄

Another Raft of Saints

So it stealthily grew, the way these things do: deftly
fingered, you might say, out of slim shadow.
Soundless.
Then densened (cloud matter, mind matter?)
till soon there were two quite rounded figures, three even,
four, distinctive, no mistake, and another...
thinking: where *will* this end –
as if 'saints' weren't enough!

The one standing tall punting this odd collection of logs
with the exact same verve
as someone you once, cruelly, fancied.
Another borne along like her own portrait, waving
distantly like a replica queen mother: 'Blessings!'
What for?
Why now?

One moment this dream-cooked unsense, conveniently
jumbly, the next this pointed tableau, looking 'meaningful';
waving the still rivery tips of long poles in your numb face,
with a raft (ha!) of such sound suggestions
up their floatily real sleeves – d'you see?

D'you *not* see?
Not want to remember perfect advice? – What
advice? but...half awake, fully
horrified at the whole notion: I mean, saints! where
in hell's name do you go from here? Just

that like so much, so many,
it can't be undreamt. ✎

Other Feet

Down suspect stairs in her bare feet. Dodgy: thunder
of a fall in waiting – a slippily turned ankle, toe nail
torn – you know, your choice to chance it,
but the naked feet
inside my head (which are an amalgam)
hurt with precaution.

And now it's flagstones, tiles, mats: the feel
of stuff not strictly speaking here.
The feel of feelings
as much as footings,
as a mixed hurt
seams through this third episode.

Conundrums
have their shoes kicked off; must
really dance now, give it some. Even the most
incidental plots are deftly laden with the a private
anticipation; the slow motion
preludes to clothes sinking, suggestively falling,
covering. And then feet,

my feet, stepping
forth, like the heroes they are
in most kinds of programme: maybe conquering
the foreign and the distant
by stealth, way before
I am done. And there ought to be time. ⁄⁄

Colours to Go

What I might call your Venus face, for the sake of no
 argument.
The softly crimson spark (peace!!) fit to light up any old
creche, tube station, check-out queue: that big grin,
 glorious
beam of attention, your own personal fire-glow
trimmed ready and shareable.

And what I'd call your [other] face – don't
make me name it. The sort when there's a crackle
of malice in the answer;
the plummy put-down
in zingy purple (if it were visible).

And the grey, shut, done, dusted face that lets people
know not to ask; a face that plainly wipes its hands after
work done deep inside your head, not a word said, OK? –
Not really.

This purely ageing face now though: *transparently* bereft
of the buzz, the hum that used to drive you just nicely
up and down supermarket aisles, unbidden.
Not even a shadow of a voice
announcing you; an other-other look on your face.

Great palette of new and gone and merely
ghosted fronts and faces, when you look – still,

underneath, in truth, no colour, no name to that
at all. When you look. ⁄⁄

True Eucalyptus

Reaching for yellow:
there's a problem right there, yellow
being happily intangible.
Spurning the unreachable tops (on planet synaesthesia),
I slide right along, hesitate over a karaoke of green
to mirror-flatter my twilight hair.

Consider the lilies: the sweet bendy feel of warm marzipan
even a rushed glance will conjure. And the chrysanths
with their small voice – shhh – like all the brooding
mothers of books, each tiny thumb of a petal making
its slight page-turning sound.
Buckets (plastic), yes, they would have clamoured
for clarion red – no other colour could have served,
in that slotted into a tight cupboard feel fashion.

And who can forgive me (I worry, worry!)
for that squelch feel of mud
at the sound of *that* accent. Best keep stumm
about things that rile ears that can't see.

Happens as it happens. Spin and turn
again: there goes the whirligig kaleidoscope
in my head, eager to rope in textures, smells –
the short-hairyness of shrill laughter,
the metal tears with their whiff of fresh snow.

Perfectly hefted to this inner landscape, this gracefully
ordered chaos: every i that exact shade
of wild primrose touched (fleetingly)
by eucalyptus. So *right*. ⧸

Being Lovely

The fractured soul of the party, life finely
divided, a mere scattery pulsation

of *me*s. – But 'You're lovely', he says,
on his leaf-thin phone (where loveliness can breed

easily, in between the bleeps) just a fraction
of an hour after me spitting spite;

a bare hour before rank bitterness; one round day
after saving almost-a-life from more than

an inkling of implosion – with that warm
rain of words I do so well.

The doing and saying and seeming
all of a time-scrunch

of shreds: nothing but glittering mirror pieces
on the surface of the ball.

Turning.

For the First Time

He looks about him at a field of grown-and-grown
question marks, tall, ready for the harvest.
A fieldful of noisy pieces that squabble poppy red hot
to fit together: a 'heart' here? a botched
doctorate there? And a soft ball still, and still, no longer
                                                    chased
because the small chaser is in permanent exile
from life. Fragments that truly hurt themselves
at their harvest; exhilarate
with their comical brilliance (his recipes
to resurrect Family gone exuberantly flat). All memorable
for their disjointedness, beforeness, chapters hanging.
Photos bereft of true attendance.
Stored wealth only so-much.
He looks more closely at the debris, hours bomb-ticking by.

He notices what must have been before, but in broken
close-ups of what it meant, then, now, ever. And confusion
breeds, like a madness spinning
on a playground now closed, deserted,
the spinner rust-squeaking its sobering protest. He stops.
Guilt as well, suddenly (arms can still reach).

He is among lost houses then, thin livelihoods snapped,
whole years overweeded and disrepaired
and all of it now like torn stuffing
ripped from the contexts
that might have supplied sense – did, did –
shouting their antidotes even then, before, even.
He looks about him stunned into knowing. ⁄⁄

Milk, of All Things

Could have been a peach, micro-furry, blushing.
Could have been the glisten and plump of cherry, the
                                    texture
of pineapple...anything. Any thing. Instead, no more
than this small runnel of milk

as it poured on, into, and rose in the bowl like a live one,
one that could cradle grain.
Cupped the fruit, completed its task – did all the doing
itself: me only an incidental pourer.

Its whiteness spelled spells. Completely
entranced. The crux of it
cleanly un-embedded, unhinged
into the open.

It made sure I'd savour milk's oddly
solid runniness with a superbly lax mind, totally
ready to be swept AWOL.
My still perfectly functioning head space said: milk.

On cereal.
In a bowl – so?
Except my free-morning mind, of some sort
of itself, chose (it? where?) to go native there,

for the merest upbeat of time; keen to dawdle beyond
what was strictly reasonable. ⁄⁄

The 13 O'Clock News

Crucially, in the space between
outbreath and in, the magic pause button: she
tries, she does. Hopes for something to come in to land

that isn't the bungled week, the husband pissed off, job
                                                                             tilting
towards capsize and mother...mothering on by a thread,
still not phoned. She tries, she does.

Holds this moment
before the bills come pouring in, before she
breathes in the particulates of more responsibilities, more

stuff untidily failed at, botched at the deskface,
ungrappled; the borderline sham everything else.
Truly.

Here, in between, she takes in the food bank kids, neighbour's
newly bust heart valve, the floods/wars/wild fires all
over the moment, this moment. –

Occasionally, just,
better things too inkling their way
into this idling space:

unstuff
that might matter, amid the dark spools
of the grip of news. Untime just presents it; no comment. ⁄⁄

The Word Child

Head spinning, differently spinning: twining strands
sifted from the most mist-headed
small notions; grasping particles not grasped at all. Surely
some common order waits to apply itself
to this mystery of crumbs and tittles?

Something of substance *will* condense,
clamped between Capital and full stop. Something *will*
take flight; find its own light, even, illumine
the thinker, this prattler of atoms: chance granules that
must follow their own coalescing grammar –

how else would there be such a thing
born, in the end? Time itself
must slither unprompted from end to beginning
of sentence, quite bypassing the latest
inner mutterings.

Acting It

What does he think when he rears, bucks, leaps
the tenth fence wholly air, causes
ructions among the ranks of the fooling?
Is this a raving invitation for us all
to follow? Each question
brings only the same answer: Joysprings! – yelled, top-of,
incongruously: showering bright fireworks
of improbability over us, the mere pedestrians here
who aren't pretending to be horses

yet...but his semblance of clowning disguises much
that could never be written down.
Shattered parts, musical fragments
of a mind so, unclearly, differently disarranged
it can only shout and twirl the truth
of itself, touching on who knows what – the only
way to grasp this particular glimmering self
is to play along, prance,
prance! Have faith. ⁄⁄

Alive

Drunk with loss – newly flung
into no-rug-underfoot country.
Where bread and pence suddenly count for something,

no, really. So that's
the meagre
leaving room for the large, at last.

And that'll be my – *my* – air
I'll be breathing out now, and the grand
feral words in it. All the way. ⫽

Staying In

She hardly means to; finds herself reaching for a
pointless glass. No evident thirst. Thoughtless
of her, but blame the spare minute clamouring,
unfulfilled, before the toot of the taxi.
She fills it anyway, the glass:
watches the tap, the water, the colourless rising.

Clear water not all that different
from clear air. She swirls, peers closely. Even if
it's a clarity more unmistakably mobile – tap on for more –
bubbling, sloshing, lapping at its boundaries with a sharp
playfulness, a splattering anger, being glass-
caught in there, in a forced going round-and-roundness.

And she reprimands herself: not the sober thoughts
of a business traveller. But continues to fill, overfill,
waterfalling and watching, overdrive nonsense of a
flipflipping finger-paddle: yes! Soooooon she'll be due
that holiday. – Time to put glass
on draining board then, taxi just drawing up.

She gives it one more
needless rinse, swishes,
in case, she thinks, as if, even, and
stares into its final
emptiness, the stopped breath of a clock.
Holds it like that.

At the door she waves, routinely, beside
her case; and when the same ever-helpful driver
leaps up the two steps and reaches (in a gesture by now
emptily repeated) she hands him
his fare – as always, before; now as never –
and just a single word drops, bursts: cancelled. ⁄⁄

Between

Thief

In a perfect world, things would float,
gravitate, sidle up.
Then grip you with all the loving fury
of mother – *possess* you – if that's the word?
Not cling to, like coats buttoned fiercely
to wrap around, wrap around, walking with, being
with, being *them*.

A scarf here; a bit of a book there; no more than a small
                                                                             thing
that may or may not have been
discarded. And one of those little soaps – it'll be...
redolent, that's the word.

I slide my all-innocence fingers along the edge
of a mere bookmark. Nose about
among oddments, fittingly.
I bide my time for the bigger stuff, with a
faint hint of falling feeling
my way towards the best of all
possible black holes: yes, a ragbag of a puzzle.

Yes, I've been eyeing up this dainty little wren
that potters about on your window sill there
for years now and years.
Granted, it would sit oddly in my house. Not
my taste at all, to be perfectly honest;
but I'd taste it
like the gourmet offerings
of a no longer foreign country
all the same.

Seen

Were your eyes grey-green for a whole seven years? Brown?
Why even remember the cheap fags we smoked the whole
hard up length of Spain, the ones called *Ducados*, why
dig that up with no effort?
Three, four unharvested fields plump with tomatoes –
we watched them so keenly: a red in decline,
a wait with question marks that weren't ours to put there.

We looked about too much. Each still hungry
for more world; forgetting even the eyes of the other.

In Switzerland, quite in passing, we sowed the seeds
of bust-ups years down the line
while appraising bare scintillas of faultlines in the rock;
so very unnoticing.

Like fluff blown along by the year's temper, we sailed:
screwed hotly, coldly didn't give a self
we hadn't yet fully assembled
from the more-or-less segments we'd been bequeathed.

Like the over-ripe fields, we'd mis-
timed ourselves, in retrospect,
and what we did inspect
was only what was laid piecemeal at our feet. – How else
did I get to mislay your eyes, recall
cut-price fags, fields of bursting red, stretching, stretching

into the distance of a different person, pale,
eyes like lakes late in the day.

Face to Face

Excuse
the threadbare talk,
the spoon-fiddling silences, plain poverty
of self-expression – my emails, I know, were much better:
                                                        lilt,
pepper, a ring to them, mental clout; there was
room for that. There always is, at a hundred arms' length.
Even a blank-screen phone call allows some creative
space
between intention
and ear, feelings and feeble lips. The barely warm
platitudes that sound sort of alright, post wine, after 10.

Excuse
the blandly flailing text
that steered so obviously clear of misunderstanding today.

Excuse
the baldness of a now gone-cold
(if time-kept) promise. Here I am.   I am.

Excuse the overly sober
humour.   Just the boiled-down-to-me me.

Excuse this brashly frightened
touching.   Excuse...

my endless over-eager echoes; your read-only smile
possibly no sign at all.   Emojis

endowed here with dead awkward
arms and legs ⁄⁄

One Hell of an Amateur Uncle

Quite visibly, you used to call your
hands and feet to heel:
arrange them better, un-indifferently.
Craving support, all too clumsily
you massaged assorted props,

though in your own faintly spade-clatter way
you still managed to stand
for the spirit of the thing.

First, the oddly angular from-bag-extracting.
Then a whole rocky road of thumby handling.
Progressing, duly pause-bound,
to a final, hasty, anyhow handing of present.

All done with a hugely question mark grace
that somehow took one's breath away,
and one's snigger impetus –
a shy man's truly joy-fumbling sacrifice.

You dropped bricks-all-over
into our comfort. And we tiptoed
through your speechlessness, all our shining greed
eclipsed by such badly wrapped feelings.
Your and our giftbow grimaces hanging off
their hinges. All tags lost, mutually.

Like that we swallowed your pain, and you ours,
every Christmas. Like medicine
that might, unaccountably, make us better
one day. An exchange so terribly fair
you *could* call it loving.

Picking a Replacement

There are the religious ones, looking blandly other-than
who might do me, except would they laugh? And no,
the reader with slant specs and a grandchild sitting so
honey-dipped will only rile the memory.
Shall I move on to the chaos of forms in the largest
canvas: maybe just a small one,
rendered harmless?
Or there's the solitary old woman
at the spinning wheel, immersed in her thoughts – but
what inexplicably perverse knots and tangles, what
tightly turned convolutions might those be...
would I be safer, now,
to look for an old lady embraced by her man,
his suitably wrinkled kindness keeping her
steady? I could find names for them both,
Matilda and her John, say, finally expunging
the Walter who left abruptly
and the other, left to spoil, who will not
be named, ever. ⁄⁄

Closer

You look at me
with such a swither of comprehension
(all sea without swish on a bare murmur of gravel)
that I feel punctured:
the precise point of it probably
escaping as we doggedly botch along
sans consonants, weave and waft and and flap
flusters of hands to aid our blurred bits of meaning, stop
to stare mid-distantly, both sage
and comic, owl-cartoonish.

We work so hard at never-minding. Willingly
heave into place another plank
of rescued sense.

Poised on needle points of silence, clueless, hands
                                              burrowed
deep into a squirm of pockets – before they come out again:

palpably
back-rubbing, visibly
arm-grasping,
where once we really would have hesitated.

Different Planet

Brave new walking stick half-pointing out some uncertain
intention...yes? no? yes?...and you're stuck to your spot,
                                                          swaying
for a whole motorists' eternity (from their point of view)
before dancing a lively crabscuttle
across their – *their* – road
with your dozen silly surplus steps at such a plainly
unnecessary (*hon-est-ly*)
diagonal slant that words fail:
all of it such a heaven-help-us near-total guess
where ACTUAL traffic is concerned!

Your wild youth is clearly painted out and over amid this
current totter, with the broadest of brushes:
wrinkles, stoop, grey-scale.

And your fraught, loud laughter-packed twenties won't
                                                          undo
that straightness of stick now either, will they.

You do realise your so sober thirties, politics and all,
aren't really helping much
with the simpleness of this crossing.
Or your whole unconventionally conceived family –
might as well not have happened, any of it.

All couldn't-care-less unguessed-at; totally, entirely,
beside the point of now (from where
others stand, rev, badmouthing, barely glance, only
just don't honk their *fucking* horn).

Maybe as long as you mind your step.
As long as your feet search. ◪

Masks Before Masks

V's warmed the whole room. Never mind his private
                                            coldness.
F could switch hers, plural, at something like rodent-
across-road speed, jaw-droppingly comical.
D, I swear, would change gears: mouth; then eyes in a deft
flitter, catching up, strapping it on. Only M's expression,
such a steady-steady kindness, stagewhispered 'mask',
made bafflement ripple through our echoes: even
smiles can cliffhang.
G's permamask likely the one face she had, has, left.

No masks here beyond the blue things for shops,
black cloth ones to have in pocket, in case. –
Just something misplaced
that seems to invite foolish rigmaroles:
      the face that abruptly leaps tracks, rips through all
                                            equilibrium;
      the dark-cloud grimace born (heavenly derailment?)
                                            out of clear blue;
      a father-alien rushing to police my forehead, frown
                                            like a finger wag;
      the scrunched *thing* that *goes on there* unbidden:
                                            fear just called out.
      Visible? hate prickles that palpably! grow.
      Tears that might fall in sympathy but prove
                                            changelings after all:
      switched for something like leather,
      sorry old cardboard,
      stiff latex.
An inexplicable crud glued to my face: week after
week since whichever witched day, month, year. (Before
masks by decree meant to take the strain.)
No chance in hell
behind any of them that I could peel

back to my old, uncomplicated, face, naked
of all this unmyselfness.

No chance now of winding back
to once upon, the quite possibly mythical beginning: day
after day in that childish sunshine
of my own skin.

Screwdriver

Nearly bit your head off there. Accumulation of the
neighbours gobbling my sleep, washing rain-rinsed, rinsed
and rinsed, work, extra mile, simply taken for granted,
ignored, nit-picked at, phoned too early, emailed too late if-
at-alled – and the lot over and over and entirely excuse-me-
please-and-sorry-less:

a whole layer on
layer sweet jammy caked construct of
anger stood there
between us.

Demanding hammer-blow behaviour. Necessitating
Gorgon face and Munch-scream mouth.
But

you managed
to get a word in first, carefully
crafted your very small question: thing of beauty, thing
totally beyond the call of duty. And of course
I assisted, stretched, stretched, reached the other
screwdriver, that and a smile that popped out of a box I
thought I'd sealed for good (or worse, *and* worse).
But I was wrong
and the thing itself, in my hand,
the gift I'd been waiting for so long: gave it back
without a moment's hesitation, a tonne of sour foolishness
                                                    lighter.

You never said 'gift'.
I never said 'thank you'. Neither of us needed words
and payment never happened.

A Burning

Without so much as a saying-so look, smallest
fraction of a tilt of the head –
but in that pause,
that slowly glow-ripening space
between one sentence and a whole new life time,
there was the beginning: in this uncoupling
of normality from the cast off selves
we'd so separately been. – You heard it too,
your pause, our growing;
the invisible gap between us closing,
even as you opened your mouth to let the next words fly
                                                                                          free
and found them gone already,
touching my lips
before leaving yours, or both, or something entirely
new that pulled your eyes after, burning the moment
to ashes
in a rush of lost time.

You swallowed.
I blinked.
Mid-lecture and in a fully witnessing auditorium –
but we both knew there was no cold amount
of now or future water
would ever quell this, totally.

Book

Should I long
for you to open, petal
by page-turning petal?
Should I not? What
will come after
the book
has been well and truly
read
you never said
and I flittered past
the question.
Your blooming, my inhaling
deeply – longer
than plain breath
would justify; hoping for
that vice versa.
Ready.
Should you. ✍

Not Saying

Four whole years and not a single one. Not one in a time of a
zillion births; none, with all my inept rustling among
bookish identifications of croakers, flappers, zoomers,
                                                    wigglers;
but there: with time zone-shifted, angle crooked
like a hither finger,
light bounced lightly
like a ball's trajectory marshalled sideways
by the mean, straight winds here
and my tread trodden to a hidden, special rhythm inherited
down the mislaid centuries in a
strange eloquence of bones –
and the calm of the
light and the angle of the hour and the deviance
of my invisible tread all conspiring: suddenly there
are hundreds; hundreds.

And tomorrow I look, and tomorrow,
and never see. Not one.

Why is that unsharable? With someone who said he fell,
literally fell off a mountain once – and waved it, me, away;
totally preserved the me-ness
of the understanding of the memory of the experience
inside his own snow globe.

Mount six-three-eight would indeed have resembled
                                                        nothing
I could have pointed to on a map.

And: you fall differently. Inevitably. With bags
I only get to pack, unpack,
not really touch with anything but fingers.

Looking For

Clear as day. Your eyes disagree. Even as you hum
warming (if off the peg) niceties. Trust me: you're still
looking for the me that could – would.
Such a picky collage memory you have there:
all cobbled and glued and spun out of
crafty titbits of my known (you think?) past and then
deftly woven together who knows how
in your head.
Threads tight enough?
No stitches dropped?

Your brush wielded with one careful eye shut and there
I stand, spade in hand, I bet, dogs
just-so at heel, a book title or two probably
flashing up above my tousle-head name, who knows –
definitely one gingerbread-cum-poacher's cottage (snug
little cradle for your feelings). Easily done. I'd even forgive
you.

But now, here, you're lost.
None of the poacher's tousle, not a sniff of the dogs, no
spade at heel. No funny gingerbread business, none.

Bright-enough (who knows where from) voice carefully
mouthing: 'nice *flat*' and 'carpets come *with it*, then?'
and your head nods, nods, understanding.

Still not choosing to see ⁄⁄

Spine Chillers

Quick brown rat across willing feet
(you phone; I run up the lane)
and *flash of gone* goes one rogue runaway train, outlaw
among hiders even in his own country.
Stick purely prop, unbrandished: wellies the thing.

My gaze scoots after, on a sliver of a wake, scuttles right
out of that door of opportunity: nothing
to see, first stars still barely on speaking terms.
Just a couple of the brassier planets applaud my effort

in the long cold of a no-moon. –
Such a shamefaced, incomplete, no help at all moon that'll
lurk, rattish, behind the house till the exact chill of four.
Then throw a thin carpet of light ahead of itself,

chew miserly into the dark. Too late then.
Right now, there might be a hundred more – your call
had that pitch – under cover of a black wait (how many
stalled breaths?) and I promised. Promised.

No matter you ignored me
the full shadow length of my time
spent, now spent, inside. Visits being hazard, stress,
question mark, yes. – Just let me fathom
this bad sky thing first: life in its simpler darkness. ⁄⁄

Strangers in Time

There'll never be a before or an after
between us now, will there, not now time's unhitched itself
    and I've never told

from its train: our feelings no longer
on track; thoughts quietly putting on their big hiking boots,
as if there could be whole worlds yet.
    maybe should never have

Let's forget where we've miles-and-miles driven to,
chattering, clueless, come back: yes, like that –
    so very nearly

each other's faces totally co-incidental now
on these twinned chairs...both keenly measuring the splat-
damage to the insect population, as we share,
    and never a day, I swear

then drop the flat unfolded into a post box that will go
nowhere in reality.
Shoulders very nearly touching. ⁄⁄

The Light in your Eyes

Bringing a mug before daybreak.
Us sitting in parallel, facing out, no matter.

A music of gestures; a moving across
the room; in your voice, no question.

Down the phone, yes: miles-crackled
and needing the urgent translation

of ages (of knowing) and still there,
no mistaking.

In twenty years' time, with you
safely under a slim tree and me gone captive,

clacking my hollow frame along in a place
I really really can't name:

still in there. ⁄⁄

Lying Somewhere Else

New bed just that: new. Habitable, in its way.
They'll find them, their old demarcation lines, in the dark,
in two minds – not battleground, exactly;
far less grappleground, not these days. Haven, not
much else to be said.
A new stamping ground for their hollow forms – their
spirits long fled: different, diverse, gone
and only the faintest drumming from a shore they know
they can't reach. (Small statues of their rare dreaming visits
are planted there, by their other lovers.)

New bed not just that; boost of new mattress too: money
well spent! And now there's a sharper glint, an intriguing
savour of difference, something begging
to begin, even at this late hour. Life's near-midnight
pompously points to all manner of pain-
dragging restrictions. But in their heads, unsummoned,
it's key and spark and Impromptu Party: a commotion
that rises to flyaway heights of imagination, fuelled
by what cards call love (and they just think of as being
into each other, whichever way).

Twelve Plates Spinning

The window pane not what it is at all.
Both boots stuck in clay here, deep into green, sharp
implement still snapping in my hands,
and I stand: stack of might-be questions impaled
on silenced tongue.
Wordlessly watch as you sit juggling
your vitally Urgent! girlfriends queued
twelve-abreast in one clearly pressing column of emails –

but no, you still
have to switch to another, equally live, bag of posts:
the photos of kids and grandkids that need to be liked
and hearted
and wowed,
before they go electronically cold,
as they will.

Back and forth
you zip on that thing, with this gleam of proficiency –
the professionalism of a therapist, counsellor
to them all. Each and every.
Nodding to yourself
even as I'm standing only a pane's thickness beyond
your catchment zone, muffle-mouthed.

But that's not what it is at all.

And the glass would never let me ask. ⁂

Gathering the Us

Snippets of belonging, magpied *con gusto* –
strictly to feather and line the way
to the future. Here's an early picking from the life line
hedgerows (still crash-landishly map-less)
achieving a first firm tick against 'crop': safe now,
past not completely obliterated. Jars, stalls even, one day –
that's to say peopled occasions. As if the world depended.

Stumbled across in this new netherworld of finds
there's a Nameless Green
with its great fall of nobody's grass-coloured gages,
great gift of a moment in full view
of near-total strangers: come, all You Passing Bewildered –
notice, question, chat an option?
Such ludicrously raw possibilities
and how to spin them.

Think: the bit-of-a-venture sour sloes yet to come.
Dream of it: that solid bottled bridge
between the gin of old – made by friends, then, there –
and the taste of a different future. Something
fluid to share with the few
icebrokenly new.

New Co-Ordinates

You tug and tug and the carefully calibrated distance
between us is instantly fire-swallowed in the roar from
your mower – apology: *our,* that is, mower.
While I try to plough into that twice-read book
we still fail to have in common.
Still,

even now roar's ebbed to harmless growl,
this newly crisp space between us
continues to waver; rucks and ripples
with a pulse all its own. To be unashamedly fanciful.
And the silver-tongued book
falls

just that little bit apart in my (still not-our) hands. No
warning, but here's a lightning bolt
louder than all your rumbling
and something tragic and comic and *itching*: a violent need
to study in close up, barbed, detail my
listing

love-torn memories of all my gone winters' stroppy
roses. How I'd cut, cut, hack them down
to the brutal ground (would you
have looked at me differently?) every year.
So there, in sum total,
it is:

what a pretty damn accurate picture I always
had in my mind – then –
what'd happen, in response,
come the cold spring. And here
the book hesitates,
whether or not to snap
shut.

Winding Up

'Files', he mumbles at her. Files to unbulge: ruthlessly
rip the old hearts out of the gone year's transactions – undo
what's reflexly done, dust the months
down, late November already.

Papers, last leaves on the path. Stuff,
all in the same category. Sweep. File. Unfile. Bin.
Weed out. Straighten. Order. Wind it up, the year –
much like cranking the stubborn old clock ready for the
next round; and he does, shows the old girl
how it's done, with a great key-fumbling fanfare, so
determined. Not that she doesn't
know.

Time to pace, fuss, round her pit of a bed:
mess of magazines, crumbs, diverse collectables
strewn and begging to be left
a while longer.
He brings cups, cleaned, scrubbed, filled precisely,
to the full measure, and she nods. Knowing.

He sighs (loud enough to entertain). He mimes weighing up
the menace of the few, very few, leaves left on the drive:
small, sneaky, doubly slippy. He points them out to her,
their acute secrets, a live and longing danger.

A moment's pause and he'll roar back into action,
action – with another stuff rotating, time
regenerating, clock-winding wave: back soon, back
soon, back soon. She knows. Watches the door being left
carefully ajar. Watches the door.

Gone. And Gone.

You inhabited my life for me
in your way.

> now the place
> they call the world
> is just a postcard
> stiff
>
> and my feelings stop
> half-way to it
>
> rebuffed
> by this repeatedly
> sharpened absence of you
> of me
>
> with my indirect
> roundabout living –
> loving –
> lacking: with you gone

I am simply missing. ⁄⁄

At a Gate

You cried – in all fairness,
it would need a whole blank page here to show that.

So my leaving was in retrospect a bright thing,
shedding light like a well-struck match, sharp
as only a slap.

Did you see the deliberate turning
of my head, going, going and gone: flown before my time?
I briefly ranked your tears a very first token (if only
observed to be paid in secret) but in truth
it was no more than a dry flash of white
across too distant a face
atop a coat identified as yours;
known, intimately, like so many things on
and around you.

Here suddenly is a giddy circling
of memories, search engine in overdrive: none of it
contains a known brand of father tears.

It is a loss, then, this too-lateness of a loss
of composure – with my head already striding off
to meet the familiar guarded barriers of the future, the so-
many closing gates, keen flights.

And who knows
if it wasn't just a snatched reflection I saw, though I
think, hope, in time pretend?
I remember.

The DNA Says

or they say the DNA says,
so who am I

to argue? This whateverpercent match, a number
served up with such a sobriety of science,

it's forgotten already in this twister of being too too
excited. – Followed in short order

by a tsunami of doubts,
a mean wave crashing against the mirror

that thunders Are You Good
Enough? To be a sister? And there my voice trails

and sinks. What does it say
in my DNA, about the best me

I might be? (And did it really take *this*
to make me ask?)

But already another wave comes rolling in,
and in, way past the innards

of the mirror. So. So. Lost for, beyond, words.
Just those fluttering letters, d and n and a.

Ghost

He did, you say, he was – and pat the corner
of the table cloth as if to smooth
the smallest memory crinkle flat, brush
something trivial away.

He used to, you say, but there he is: peering over your
shoulder in his old uniform, emphatic chin, expensively
framed. The sun glints on his first glasses
as you speak, nod, rake gently through his past: titbits
to offer the visitor.

You pour him out with the tea,
this ghost. Serve him proudly
with the biscuits. No more than a mumble
about yourself.

Your health (oh, that) clattered over with the cups and
saucers, needless spoons, just clearing away.

And then the door goes and there's the bent-over, the
unframed version. With the now much thicker glasses.
'Visitor?' and he enters with a rawness of presence honed
over decades of thin marriage. – I can only watch you pale

and pale further from view, go quietly greyscale
till I can no longer imagine you'd ever, rudely, eat – never
mind snatching a quick mirror image
on the way out. ∕∕

The Safety of No-One

X will do her just fine, at a distance: typically pulling away
with the eagerness of a dog to be gone.

X comes back for meals, as they do, and she cooks them
like glad sacrifices, eager to be gone, at her task.

X leaves. There is someone, she knows,
suspects, ignores, knowingly.

X has no attributes to speak of when he's gone. And when
he's really gone, that sort of ex, the exness of

X is so lacking in any handles that would raise him again
into her mind that she wonders at the beauty of the

vacuum she had called her own. The simple place of it:
irreplaceable. And when she is gone, joining

X under her own obligatory cross, they will remember her
as someone who bore a great burden with such grace. ⫽

Never Saw Me

Think you'd jostle past me unseeing, determinedly
purchase-struck: still the hurter ('bully' was never
said), still the wordless elbow?

Think you'd just pop out of this vague smudge of people,
quick upheave of past, breeze past, dismissed?

Not, as it happens, before I clock the same old
finger-pointing set of the chin, the same
half-shuttered eyes, proud poise of the head on a
strong as anything neck (never really any quarter given):
and yes, it's instant tongue-stuck recognition, on my part.

But there beside you that newly old daughter of yours –
reshuffling my irritated memory entirely –
is twice as tall-shouldering by your side,
loping a doubtless inherited
half stride ahead, hair bouncing
in that ruthless way grown-daughter hair has
(and boy, does she need it).

Passing by so very professionally not seeing. Doing, as
ever, that being intensely with – the *with,* or not,
a hundred percent contingent on life's every
random (literally) pimple.
    Every one of them still
    burnt, in, deep, bloody, red. //

Voiceless

Her hand flies up: as if to cup a tender bit, stroke
an old wound, check, and again.
Flutters among less vivid symptoms.

Her halting fingers tiptoe across a desert
of throat: strictly, strictly in time to a What? or a
What! from him, in one of his guises (such a skilled

shouter, such a sly demander, faultless
inquisitor, a man home on the dot,
never not). And always it falls to her fingers

to draw the answers, thumbs to furnish
exclamation marks. Whole pointed, fiddled, fidgeted
sentences are tapped, pronto; quickly rubbed out;

repeated on this live parchment of neck. And again: just
get it!...*get it* you...*stupid* bitch! Again
and again nothing leaps from her throat, nothing

but the cautious hiccups, voiceless winces
when an index stumbles, scrabbles
at a still talkative bruise.

Entire finger stories there: soft tips flutter to outline;
nails draw firm hints on skin. Skin pinched
and held has to serve – doors closed altogether now:

last secure prop for breath's safe control.
Her little nods rarely interfere with her eloquent
handiwork. Her fast collecting, unread, works. ⁄⁄

The Sand Underfoot

Your implacable demands so softly
impressed: deliberate rhythm, silent repetition,
feet placed with immense care.

Me, my unspoken resentment
firmly drills down. Sound muted, and stand-in feet
pound out what tongue won't.

The beach – protagonist here – still proving as long
as a marriage might last: the sink and
resist of sand become our anchor

amid the brave unthought.
Watching the waves find solid ground,
we hold hands unprepared –

as if they were objects
found and ultimately far too
puzzling.

Don't Shoot the Owl

Me, still me, still struck dumb by the rushed relocation,
trying hard already to fit, knit myself
into the fabric of this back to front lane – five new
clearly not-gardening neighbours –
gangling trees, ragged lawns, magpies aplod,
thump of car stereo, thump in my temple and tongue
held...smile before those doors close!

Early nights here, after all that.
Punctured, like something thinly precious,
by owl.

And the next-day curses directed at sky, wood, it
and me, plain enough. I've brought it, no doubt: treasured
life luggage, owls and all their close hang-gliding ilk.
Not much else of worth to take
from this place to that – memories, winged images.

Doves on those early, verboten balconies, gentling the
                                                        threat;
owls ably parenting a bed-bound scardy-cat;
the gangs of bold-brained magpies, with their hoarse gossip
of bright miracles soon. Always there; always where

I go, rightly, properly, there they'll pop up: doves,
owls, magpies et al, among the not-gardening neighbours
and their musicky noise, and my poise, and theirs,
interleaved, twined, twinned in so

many respects. So don't curse it, don't
shoot down the owl (even in a quick manner of speaking).

The Real Rat

It smiled at me, even
as I stood with bloody hatchet
raised, butcher-like, murderous.
                        It smiled
beside my bed, in my TV chair, perched all lively
on the toilet seat, horribly intimate...smiled till I felt
my hatchet arm sink to a level
so deep

below anything in properly metered life
it was a new place
altogether; a space where we
could. Definitely. It
and me.
                        No use at all
calling it delusiondreamfantasyblah – explain
away nothing, in reality.
The shining clarity of it, straight-up,
all there in that smile
                        and
it persists, insists, resists
any rejoining. ⁄⁄

Earth People

Walls and walls *and* walls before you ever hit the edge
of town, inhale that Edginess. Give it the doubtful stare.
Genuine tarmac treaders,
that's us alright, night timers without
the real star stuff:
our skyscapes hemmed/redrawn/quartered
by buildings, buildings, buildings.

But been there, postcard, T-shirtless holiday
among green stuff and views, *paths*.

All in the same vein, really: too tightly
engineered to *happen*. Teetering sun-slathered
nowhere near grown-up precipices, nowhere
near the life-rattling margins
of 'civilisation'.
Comical or what?

Can we help ourselves, at all, flapping
maps/stout guide books at flies just a tad...too big?

But: irony – as soon as we're back,
safe behind our double (and some) locked doors,
and TV hurricane worshippers R Defo Us again.
Absurdly true
to one of our simplest hungers.

Somewhere in the gut of things
still managing to scream
Lies! at the primping and packaging,
the pre-pre-booked amazements,
planned weather. ∕∕

Other Others

    Impossible to hear what on
    earth they're saying:
there's a fly-flail of arms, there's a bedazzle of mouths
foreign and cavernous and with a noise of cold rapids –
then this collective seizure of shrugs...what?!...
a seething tumble, a squirming
mass, personal spaces all askew there:
horseplay or spat?
No idea.

    Impossible to see what on
    earth they're about:
a babbling stew of rubber vowels,
pops and pings and frankly bastard consonants,
a stab of knife-pitch shrieks and great
splatters of laughter – and then the odd growl like
night itself and
really: who'd
want to know?

    No: leaving it
    to others to address
    The Problem. ⁄⁄

A Whole Load of Space

See how they calibrate. See how their mouths calculate
each word, modulate tone, length, roundness of each
careful-now vowel, the dithery lingering.

I know my jaw is too (*how* too?) slack, a slant that
'shouldn't be there' to my eyes
but no need for the tape to come out, measuring
length and width of every one of my words, weighing up
every emphasis (I *get* long words, see).
None of us are infectious, just so you know. Being
different ain't catching.

Old man there with his scabby clothes, bad skin, smell
from another planet; hushed woman with her
complicated hair grown on an unknown continent and
her too many bright dark children; a lost mutterer.
All with the special speaking-to needs
of those standing out, apart:
patience consumers; carefulness requirers; tainting
the usual discourse with something like speed bumps.

The scuff-faced boy with his well torn top
probably from the dank maw of a bin
politely addressed by a smart guy in *his* fashion-torn,
card-flickingly paid for...in tones as if it needed a verbal
sand bag there.

All those finely judged (judged!) spaces.
Not visible exactly – 'don't be rude' right? –
just hanging thick in the air. 'I get off here for...?'
mumbled in what's classed
as an out-land-ish accent, and the answer,
slow in coming, has that strange finish to it,
that buffer sound, an arm's length cadence.

The ring of distance.
You could write a symphony in that key, sad, tragic, operatic maybe – I mean, when all is said, dying swans would get more of a cosy reception.
On a half empty bus. ⌐

Rules

He gets it, the waxing and waning, the in breaths and out.
In: clamped, hard, shackled, shut; and out: airy rush,
free to go. Free to stay. Be.

They, it – *that* – keeps him wrung tight, taut,
like a months old bud. Then, pooff, it expands: safe here.
Minus the sharp-eyed crowding past. Minus violence
pouring out of a hundred mouthy windows. Nothing
to jab at (even the most immaterial) wounds. Nothing
                                                                    remotely.
Up and down the street there's only innocence of intent,
a tree or two, new, still gangly, zero threat –
the whole streetscape a sponge to absorb him, all of him,
a safe as safe expanse: outbreath.
And a fine fat flat pause.

Next corner, and it's on again, the eyes-down edging past
ducking the volleys of shouts (anon.), elbows (ditto),
all sparking yet another panic's worth of constricting
thoughts
that make him breathe in,
keep in,
hold in.
Small and tight again and self-self-self-contained.

No one's stride loose here,
no one's face open for the business
of caring a jot – throughout,
the rules of a monstrous moon apply:
wax,
wane,
watch,
whatever,
whoever.
All of it.

Counting

Interlopers. Precisely what they are: every evening
scamper off to their little enclosures – 'homes', then.
Locked, bolted, windows a curtained blank, eyeless.

Magic switch, and the back streets open: skip-scurrying
prowlers, nameless mates, bag carriers with the odd dog –
some of the sanest people, out they pour.

And it's a neighbourhood newly hatched, a differently
normal feel to it. Cold itself in a much meaner hurry here.
Darkness too: grows bigger AND BIGGER ears

despite the far too many shadows round about
being (not entirely grudgingly) family.
Only sort.

Then the nightly circus of scraps and jostling and sharing
and thieving till finally, finally:
together, we work at sleep. – Dawn before you know it.

Best be off, find some half-way kosher place,
some doubly hard space (fat fucking insult, more like).
My 108th blanket day, I would have said, if

you'd asked. – It'd add something, you might want to know,
to the blingy round and
roundness of your £2 coin if you did. ⁄⁄

Blue Fingers

Scrupulously, I don't stare. Even sidelong.
All best bus crush reticence: ask not a word.
Hey, how come your fingers are blue? never said. Still,

I can see how you're admiring them –
sat there all quiet on your ownsome – mother frowningly
phone bound (sworn prisoner of distant communication).

The only kid among busing oldies, left to your doubtless
grand (invisible) solo performance
behind a sparse princess wall. I see that. No pretty pink

touch-me-not roses either. Just the clear stop-there
glass of evolving (snatched glimpse?) suspicion: living,
growing, hard thorns,

ever more.
And glances must shrink,
heart contract, run to a different blueness:

cold. Absolute,
crucial. Disconnect.
Seems all our clever wiredness is useless. ⁄⁄

Today, in the Plaza

Tumbling ahead of dad, mum, nan,
he comes shooting out of that shop mouth

like a small flash flood of supercharged words
still lost for their breath;

mutely, clamps doubly fierce arms
around his huge box-bound treasure.

His unhollered joy, bolt-from-the-sky,
slices clean into the dull of my day,

punctures it: leaves a tower of haunting, a biting
sizzle, splinters in my memory.

The same feral wave crashes through him with no
pause – nothing gets noted, filed.

Soon, on the next small tide,
we'll part company again, harmlessly drift

continents apart.

Other anthologies and collections available from Stairwell Books

Lunch on a Green Ledge	Stella Davis
there is an england	Harry Gallagher
Iconic Tattoo	Richard Harries
Fatherhood	CS Fuqua
Herdsmenization	Ngozi Olivia Osuoha
On the Other Side of the Beach, Light	Daniel Skyle
Words from a Distance	Ed. Amina Alyal, Judi Sissons
All My Hands Are Now Empty	Linda Baker
Fractured	Shannon O'Neill
Unknown	Anna Rose James, Elizabeth Chadwick Pywell
When We Wake We Think We're Whalers from Eden	Bob Beagrie
Awakening	Richard Harries
A Stray Dog, Following	Greg Quiery
Blue Saxophone	Rosemary Palmeira
Steel Tipped Snowflakes 1	Izzy Rhiannon Jones, Becca Miles, Laura Voivodeship
Where the Hares Are	John Gilham
The Glass King	Gary Allen
A Thing of Beauty Is a Joy Forever	Don Walls
Gooseberries	Val Horner
Poetry for the Newly Single 40 Something	Maria Stephenson
Northern Lights	Harry Gallagher
Nothing Is Meant to be Broken	Mark Connors
Heading for the Hills	Gillian Byrom-Smith
More Exhibitionism	Ed. Glen Taylor
The Beggars of York	Don Walls
Lodestone	Hannah Stone
Unsettled Accounts	Tony Lucas
Learning to Breathe	John Gilham
New Crops from Old Fields	Ed. Oz Hardwick
The Ordinariness of Parrots	Amina Alyal
Homeless	Ed. Ross Raisin
Sometimes I Fly	Tim Goldthorpe
Somewhere Else	Don Walls
Still Life with Wine and Cheese	Ed. Rose Drew, Alan Gillott

For further information please contact rose@stairwellbooks.com

www.stairwellbooks.co.uk
@stairwellbooks

www.ingramcontent.com/pod-product-compliance
Lightning Source LLC
Chambersburg PA
CBHW031206090426
42736CB00009B/799